The Autobiography

of Poverty

The Autobiography of Poverty

My Childhood in Poem

The Autobiography
of Poverty

My Life in Poem

Doris Wellington

The Autobiography of Poverty: My childhood in Poem

Doris Wellington © 2018
Dwelling Places Worldwide
home of books and letters by Doris Wellington
Georgia

Unless otherwise noted
All scriptures are taken from King James Version of the Bible
First US Copyright printing, 2018
CreateSpace Independent Publishing Platform
North Charleston, SC, USA
Available on Amazon.com
and other online outlets

Second Printing 2023

ISBN-13:978-0-692-13615-7
ISBN-10: 0692136150

Cover Design
Doris Wellington

Dedication

I dedicate this work to my mother, Hattie Vance Wellington, with whom I shared a full life of mutual love, admiration and joy for poetry. She not only taught me how to live, she showed me how to live with dignity and respect of humanity—that it doesn't matter how many times life knocks you down, you can get up dancing if you don't give up.

I honor you for what you gave me—earth life, unconditional love, nurture of soul, faith in God, freedom to dream, wings to fly, and the unbridled force of your determined resolve. This is your enduring legacy, which I don't take lightly.

You're home now...

I dedicate this book to anyone who has overcome and continues to overcome tremendous odds—resilient—steadfast ---determined to leave a legacy of a bold unstoppable warrior in the face of opposition.

Inside This Volume

Foreword—7

Introduction—8-13

Everybody's Talking about Hattie Mae's Children—14-15

530 Manchester—16-17

An Unlikely Ally—18-25

Confessions of the Shotgun House—26-36

Hunger--37

Cheating Poverty—38-40

Banquet of the Dispossessed—41-52

The Eugenics Conspiracy—53-55

Cotton: the Coronation of the American Dream—56-66

The Food that Angels Brings—67

Sell or Discard by Friday—68

Butterflies and Bean Cans—69-70

Library Rules—71-73

Shadows on the Ceiling—74-91

Places Called Home—92-93

Ritual of Humiliation—94-95

Blackberry Dreams—96-98

The Parable of One—99-101

Everybody's Talking about Hattie Mae's Children Again—102-106

Foreword

In her compelling work, *The Autobiography of Poverty: My Childhood in Poem*, author, Doris Wellington interweaves graphic poetic narratives that open the portal to a symphonic expose in which those least expected battle and overcome the crucibles of poverty—one of the most devastating of all human experiences. Dramatic literary language extracts from the severity of her childhood reality and invites readers into a world of transparent vulnerabilities, challenges, and distresses.

She is not afraid to confront what some attempt to paint and pass off as an irreversible affliction that disfigures an otherwise perfect society. However, the author points out that it is not the poor who are the stain on society; rather those who close their eyes, pull down their shutters, in hope that the poor will go away—forgetting that when we turn a deaf ear or a cold heart against human suffering—whatever the plight, we have become the affliction among the afflicted we hate—the evil that stains society with indifference.

I have collaborated with author, Doris Wellington on numerous exhibitions of verse and aesthetics—a woman of letters who weaves the metaphysical and the phenomenology in a tapestry of hope for all who dare cross the chasm to hear her voice and experience the endowment of the divinity of God. Deep within this woman of wisdom, she births the gift of the aesthetic experience to elevate the one and bring closer the other. She is as raw, passionate, genuine and infectious in her work as all prophets who aspire to transform worlds by the very nature of their gift. This Autobiography is no exception.

Nancy Bookhart
MFA, University of GA, Athens
PhD
Philosophy and Aesthetics
Institute for Doctoral Studies in the Visual Arts

Introduction

Through the Eyes of a Teenage Daughter

I begin this poetic expose about my life in poverty at 530 Manchester Street because it is one of the most vivid memories I have of my mother and the personification of the strength of her character and my perception of her womanhood as a teenage daughter growing up poor in North Carolina. I do not suggest that my mother was perfect or that my father was not there; I do not even suggest that she was a perfect nurturer or that my father was no nurturer at all; only that her effect on how I overcame in poverty was more positive than his, and that, where earth mothers are concerned, there was none greater to possess in an environment such as mine.

In spite of the poverty I endured during the three or so teenage years I lived in the three-room shotgun house—it had the most profound effect on my understanding of my mother. There are memories of her during earlier years that are fleeting, and somewhat amorphous—specific things that speak to her constancy as a mother, but not necessarily her buoyancy as a woman, which I had no concept of as a child. I would later come to understand and appreciate those formative years of observing her as the foundation for everything that I have come to appreciate in her as a woman.

I remember at least ten addresses before Manchester—my mother and father going wherever they would allow a family of twelve; and although the moving was challenging, Mudd would always find a way to minimize the effect moving had on education and life in general.

She was my mother and she was there—stringing clothes on the back clothesline, washing in a sable pot, stitching dresses with her hands for my sisters and me, ironing on a legless ironing board propped between two ladderback chairs, stirring the fire to cook flour bread on top of a wood burning heater to eat with Karo Syrup or syrup made from sugar, preparing ten paper bags from IGA for Christmas morning surprises, making Tea Cakes and homemade banana pudding when we could afford it, and yes, singing, praying, and moaning in the bathroom as I watched through the small crack of the door that could not lock because like nothing else in life, poverty exposes deficiencies even behind closed doors.

Happy Hill was a strange name for those cast aside by the disillusionment of happiness. We lived in the kind of complex where four families lived on each floor of the three-level building. It was there I sat by the Formica top table, watching Mudd cook—a mere six-year-old creating words on brown paper bags, which I would later accuse Webster of stealing. In the third grade I sat for Ms. Blue's Class at Sam Vick—Mudd told me how proud she was of me. In the fourth grade, I fainted in Ms. Hood's class and Mudd rushed to the school to see to my crisis—it was probably a hunger headache.

I remember the Barbecue Shack where Mudd worked a while when we lived on Lincoln Street. She was a dishwasher. She would bring home gallon Mason jars of tenderloins and cabbages that could've only come from the world of God. OMGGG—that's O my Goodness, Gracious God!! One of those hot days, she came dangerously close to losing her fingers in a turning fan. As she went to adjust it, her hand got caught and she lost the tips of three of her fingers on the right hand. For pain and suffering, she was given a meager nine dollars, and against dad's counsel to the contrary, she signed a document waiving her rights to any future claims for damages. Since that day, I noticed she always fiddled with the fingers she damaged in the fan.

I'm not sure if they bothered her or if they were a constant reminder of what she had lost feeding her children or perhaps, not listening to dad.

While still on Lincoln Street and attending Elvie Street Elementary, I got my first ministry challenge in fifth grade—I was eleven. One of my classmates had a seizure while Mrs. Bynum was out of the room. I got on my knees and placed my hand under her head the way I'd seen Mudd do when my sister had a choking spasm. I'm not certain what I said to her—I just know she yielded to my quiet authority. When I got home I shared the incident with mom and she praised my courage for stepping forward.

But, it was in this house on Manchester Street surrounded by Plaster of Paris school projects, stale sweet buns and rolls from the corner bakery on Pender and Nash, and poor folk furniture from wherever it was sold or passed on, that I began to form a picture of this powerful woman as she instilled invaluable life lessons that shaped my resistance to mediocrity. Through every challenge in her life, she has modeled grace, even in the midst of everything that seemed hopeless.

Under the listless quiet of poverty, the writer in me began to emerge and right there in the midst of abject lack, I penned my first real poem—A Lover's faith—I was just out of sixth grade. I sent it to one of those magazines that advertise for songs, and like all aspiring artists, I was elated when the magazine informed me I was accepted—ignorant of the fact that it probably accepted everyone. But, it didn't matter, I showed the letter to Mudd and she congratulated me on my first real poem. That was it, poor or not, I would someday be a writer and I would go to Hollywood and write film scripts about amazing people who had been faced with insurmountable odds and still had emerged triumphant. It was a dream born in a world where dreams die in the womb, but Mudd made them seem possible; and so, I believed and followed her. She would walk around the house singing, shouting and speaking her up tempo melodies about the goodness of God.

Here, I waltzed for the first time as a fairy princess in a school production before the entire student body. It wasn't the dance I feared most—it was not getting an elegant dress to look the part. I don't remember how the dress came to be; perhaps it was sent in a box from "up the road" meaning New York or New Jersey by one of mom's aunts; perhaps, it came from a thrift store or one of the ladies mom cleaned for. I don't recall—all I know is when I stepped into the spotlight to do my waltz—no one outshined me.

The dress was a floral blue and white organza, draped across the shoulders, fitted at the waist and cascading about the knees. I wore white pumps. For once, my hair was manageable in an upswing bun. A single strand of precious pearls adorned my neck—from where, I don't know. I was the fairytale princess and mom was my fairytale godmother—that's all that mattered.

On Manchester, I evolved as the mysterious phantom lover—penning romantic love poems under the pseudonym, "The Spoiler." It was the fantasy that kept me from dying from the pathogenic entrapment of poverty. My sisters, Nancy, Frances and Louise would steal my poetry and present it to their boyfriends as their own. I caught at least one of them in the act but I didn't care. I was glad they liked it.

It was in the front yard on Manchester where mom snatched the gun from my uncle's artificial hook arm and threw it under the wood frame house because he handled it without regard for her children. That day she told my father in no uncertain terms that if he continued to act like a child, she was going to leave him with the follies of him and his brother.

Here, under the eyes of nosey, inquisitive neighbors, she carried her eleventh child six years removed from her last pregnancy—denied government assistance because she refused to submit to voluntary sterilization. And while my father was away looking for better work in Alexandria, Virginia, my mother staved off the advances of her old, foul neighbor who tried to tempt her into bed brandishing his bank roll while she strung clothes on the back clothesline.

Here, she attended to the puberty of five girls with no man around to help steer them out of the path of predators, and none of them turned up pregnant as it was predicted. There were ten children in school and a lot to be concerned about without a father or husband around to help balance the load. So to direct our attention to more positive matters, she made church and school a priority. To keep us out of the eye of the storm, we weren't allowed to wander the neighborhood, stay overnight with friends, or have boyfriend running in and out the house or hanging around porch talking mindless chit-chat.

Manchester was where Mudd juggled worked as a domestic servant, a factory worker, and a fieldhand to feed and clothe us. I witnessed that with my own eyes as clearly as I could see straight from the front to the back of the shotgun house. After working all week and sometimes Saturday, she would prop up that old legless ironing board between two ladder-back chairs and prepared us for Sunday. And on Sunday mornings, we became a caravan of socks and shoes moving in harmony toward Piney Grove Freewill Baptist Church in Wilson, North Carolina. Or one of the free Sunday taxis would pick us up for church.

It was there, behind Pender Street, in a place we called the schoolyard where I learned to respect her voice as authoritative and uncompromising. Whether it was rebuke or instructions, comfort or encouragement, laughter or joy, she was always concerned about steering us out of the path of hurt and danger or the danger of mediocrity. If we wanted anything other than poverty, we would have to pay little or no attention to those who had settled in it.

Here I finished sixth grade at Elvie Street after we returned from the country working for a Caucasian man who owned a farm. When I graduated seventh grade, mom bought me a beautiful white dress and allowed me to wear stockings with garters and pumps.

Two years later, I entered Charles H. Darden High School. And for the first time, I began to understand how hard Mudd worked to assure that our poverty was not exposed. But however noble her efforts, they were not enough—the deficiencies began to ooze and those around us saw. Even one of my teachers pointed out mine during homeroom in the presence of two hot Varsity football players. "No one could be more attractive than Wellington if she fixed herself up." Perhaps it was a compliment, but for me, it was an unnecessary exposure to shame.

Here, my own maturity began to take shape and with that the lens of my perception began to focus on my mother's womanhood, which included everything she was. She was more than just my mother.

When I wanted to drop out of Darden High in the ninth grade because I was tired of going to school hungry and humiliated by meanness; it was there—on the front porch of 530 Manchester Street where Mudd reminded me that she had dropped out of school and married at seventeen to get away from home and that no child of hers was going to drop out in any grade for any reason if she could help it—hungry or not. So, to make ends meet, the older children were expected to help out in the fields in the summer tobacco season. In the fall, we were kept out with the excuse that we were picking cotton for book fee and clothes, which never materialized until or unless we were caught up with rent, food, and utilities. These memories I hold in the highest regard because they created the template I use to conquer all of life even to this moment. My mother has passed on to the heaven she believed exists and I'm left here to fulfill my place in life holding fast to the lessons she taught me while facing the challenges of poverty.

Everybody's Talking about Hattie Mae's Children

Hattie Mae
Got good children
Manners
Smarts
And good looking

But they won't get far

Too much against them
(Period)
Their father drinks
With the worst of louses
Their mother scrubs floors
In white women houses

Thirteen mouths to feed
on menial labor
Picking cotton
Putting in tobacco
Trying to make it

Books
Clothes
Shoes to buy
Nothing left
to cultivate the mind

She just got too many
(Period
The girls will turn up pregnant
The boys in trouble
Or jail
The fields won't turn out
Geniuses
Church won't preclude
Welfare

Forget about college
Or becoming anything
Worthwhile
And that's a shame
She's got good children
But good won't bail them out
(And that's that)

The Autobiography of Poverty

530 Manchester

Collard greens
Cornbread
Butter—no biscuits
Mr. Red
Sleepy
Moonshine Whiskey
Snuff dipping
Tobacco chewing
Dirt at a dime
Spitters
Whippers
Yunguns crying
Street gangs
Catch a Girl
Six to five
Woodman
Crack'lins
Skins and wine

Backyard brawling
Monkey fitting
Mammies hollering
Cleaning chit'lins
Hopscotch
Jump rope
Jack rocks
Marbles

Killing
Stealing
Liquor bottles

Hunger
Hurting
Shooting jive
Roots
Roaches
Surplus lines

Poverty

Unapologetic

An Unlikely Ally

Can you guess my age
I've fought wars
no one my age should have fought
and won
civil war and civil rights
the revolutionary struggle
for identity
in these united states

I've been held captive
by the dreams of the sharecroppers
labor sold to the highest bidder
putting in tobacco
pulling cucumbers
picking cotton
just to pay the rent
to live in a shotgun house
one more month
at seven dollars and fifty cents

The Autobiography of Poverty

I've been hungry more times
then I care to remember
eating bland blackeye peas
and chicken gizzards

Evicted for no reason
except
I was just one
among too many
undesirables

I've walked to school
in shoes too small
baby toes exposed by holes
cut to fit the feet
attacked by the elements
frozen stiff by winter's breath
unsympathetic

Do you know what it's like
to wear grown up clothes at ten
made for women who wear perfume
and bras
and girdles to hide
their bulging guts
when all you want
is to be looked upon
like boys look at girls
who wear clothes their age
waiting for that first wink

The Autobiography of Poverty

Instead of a backward blouse
to cover the shame of life
bequeathed to those
deemed
less likely to survive
who know their worth
but rarely given the chance
to contemplate the future
cause they're too busy
overcoming
what others take for granted

Clean water
a hot meal
a roof that does not leak
bed springs
that don't bite
floors without snake holes
a working toilet
or paper goods
instead of cornhusk

Have you ever combed the stench
of somebody's trash
to find anything
to feed upon
or eaten candy
from the ground
trampled beneath the feet

Or clay dirt
and ice cubes
as delusionary substitutes
for food
to stop the pang of hunger
or the pain of disease
to long one moment of heat
that fills the cold damp of
winters with warmth

Warmth
that covers the deepest sorrow
and pushes back the veil
to summon laughter

Laughter that conceals
the pounding
heartbeat
of mourning

Laughter
soaring with eagles
sauntering like peacocks
falling and
getting up
falling again
and getting up
swelling full
like the wind
blowing
boisterously

The Autobiography of Poverty

Laughter
untamed
cyclical
carried on the backbone of slaves
like African mothers
bore nations
without the honor of kings
laughing
miscarrying seed
from stress
and restless toil
yet still pregnant
with possibility

Laughing about anything
to keep from crying
playing laughing games
to keep from dying
Catch a Girl, Kiss a Boy
Freeze
and Stand
Pat-a-cake
Pat-a-cake
Baker's Man
Hopscotch
Double Dutch
Miss Mary Mack
Marbles
string art
the Poetry
of gods

Silly putty
faces in mud
tempers in a rage
"Mom!
Mr. Slim is at the door
with fish on a string"

Peeping through
cardboard
windows
to determine
the risk
of laughing
at Mr. Slim
henpecked
by Miss Lizzie
          Or Mr. Red
hocking and spitting
snuff in a filthy tin can
his peeping Tom
perverted lisp
pronouncing "thee"
instead of she

Nit Nat Nu
and Sleepy
quarreling
in the alley
one talking
through Cold Duck
for the other everything sounds like N
through her nasal passage

The Autobiography of Poverty

If Neepy
non't
neeve nee anone
n'iam
nonna
Nick nis nass
Sleepy
doesn't answer a word
just staggers
cussing
and swearing

Woman
if you had
some damn teeth
you'd still be
ugly as hell
But since I know
you broke as this fifth
I have nothing
to fear

We're laughing
so hard
we're crying
head rattling
into spasms
knowing
that there
is nothing to eat
but flour bread
and sugar syrup

Knowing that Mudd
just rejected
fish on a string
because there was no way
to keep or cook them
even after cleaned

Still laughing
defying the odds
staring her in the face
generations waiting
in her womb
born in iniquity
shaped by faith

Together
they laugh
until they burst wide with dance
stomach tied in knots
with joy
and new strength
from an unlikely ally

Confessions of the Shotgun House

May 7, 2018

I'm less than 650 square feet of existence
In plywood
planks really
center blocks
uphold
and keep me steady

I am bland
colorless
uninteresting to the eye
no one sees me
or seeks me out

Situated on the alley side
between 528 and 532
I am 530A Manchester
genetically linked to 530B
my life partner
in slum dwelling
impoverished
misery

The Autobiography of Poverty

Consisting of three rooms
with no distinctive identity
known by the inhabitants
simply as
the front room
middle
and the kitchen

Where a bathroom is tucked
conspicuously
without shame
in direct sightline
from front to back
with a chimney
for a wood burning
pot belly stove
for warmth
and cooking
when there is no gas
or electricity

My floors are wood
but not in the sense
of enviable vintage
for there are holes
in the boards
inviting the
contemptible

The Autobiography of Poverty

Rodents and rats
snakes
bugs
and spiders
on torrid
summer days

There are two steps
to the front
and back porch
where one
perhaps two
might sit
if the notion
strikes

Each room
has a window
the front door has panes
to stand and gaze
at the plight of neighbors
or listen
with intense disbelief
at the strain of life

Announcing itself
feverishly
in the services it renders
to survive

"Woodman!"
"Iceman!"
"Candy man!"
"Crack'lins!'
"Watermelons!"
"Tomatoes"!
"Beans!"
"Kindling"!

Regrettably
I do not recall
all the families
I have sheltered
except
with some measure of pleasure
I remember them

For three years
I would cover their days
beneath the roof
of hunger
spasms
and empty
shame
without understanding
what they yearned
beyond survival

Or even if
they even dared
to wish and dream
in their despair
apart from that
I did not know
the depth
of power
behind my walls

Preachers
Prophets
Diviners of dreams
Politicians
and Poets
Philosophical
thinkers
came
from Allen Newbern
under the cover of dark
like slaves escaping
drenched in the hope
of castaways
looking for Jericho

Thirty-six months
they danced
and pranced
in the frolic of fools

Half-fed
half-nourished
Half-clothed
and-shoed

Ten children slept
in the middle room
no partition drawn
privacy left
to the moral standards
taught
by the watchwoman
they called
Mudd

Boys on one bed
girls on the other
legs flung across bodies
like Siamese twins
connected at birth
dreaming one dream
caressing one hope
bound
by one prophesy

"I'm having these children for God"
she whispered
to her night work
a makeshift ironing board
propped
between two ladder back chairs
bore her witness
"These are not my children
they 're Yours"

"Feed them, Lord
I have no money
no education
to speak of with pride
and their father
left school
to tend the farm
has even less than I"

Then I knew
that my assignment
however long
was to hide their destinies
from premature
discovery
or dying
in the womb

I made a vow
to keep their secrets
from imps
and demons
on leave from hell
judgmental
friends
and bigot strangers
need not ask
I would not tell

There
under the drudge of suffering
I hid the future
from the sinister scourge
and drunken rage
of Satan's wrath

Spewing his anger
into hollow empty threats
that bore him no victims

The gun was raised
but the bullet fell limp
the jealous contempt
of the unscrupulous
set its trap
lying in wait for girls
who'd come of age

And the criminal
partnership
of the son
who took the wrong friend
Into his bosom
but was spared
a juvenile record
because the watchwoman
pleaded with the judge
and built a hedge
around his puberty

The Autobiography of Poverty

You will not become
a juvenile delinquent
quell your temptation
to die in winter

You will not be a dropout
for lack of food
feed your hunger hope
to satisfy
the famish of soul

You will not fail
for lack of books
command your God brain
to attention
and assert your right
to education

You will not summon
poverty
as an excuse for failure
declare your power to change
not to conform
to circumstance

One by one
I saw the giants lunge
and slain
by a sling shot
formed
by deliberate
acts of defiance

And the fervent
passionate invocations
of Rachel's weeping
for her children

On and on
stitching
engraving
carving
resistance
to nothingness
and nobodiness
to the core
of their existence

If by chance
they swallowed indifference
purposely
or accidentally
she performed
her ritual of exorcism
"The Devil is a Liar!!
Resist him!"
she wailed
until they vomited
the folly of
paupers' mourning
and reclaimed their strength
to walk undaunted
in the valley
of the shadows of death

The Autobiography of Poverty

I saw
I heard
and I knew
that the barren
infertile ground

where they were planted
would not
could not
abort
where hope
and dreams
are nourished
'til born
And love
their greatest
ally

Hunger

Peanut Butter on paper bags
greasy
running

Flour bread
no butter
on an empty stomach
churning

Crushed ice
going down
a hollow empty trail
stumbling

Powder eggs
undefined in purpose
crumbling

H U N G E R
lingering
undisturbed

again

Cheating Poverty

Today I cried
because of the things
poverty steals

There are no pictures
to savor the memories
of childhood
at twelve

The journey through puberty
my first dance
a proud seventh grader
waltzing
with Chantz

No pictures of me
at Elvie Street
when I first wore stockings
veiled
feet
for rites of passage

Poverty
stole
and stole
and stole

until there was nothing left
but pain
of soul

And memories
stored in places
where the thief
couldn't steal

Where pictures
won't bend
or colors bleed
and fade

Secured in vaults
with hidden keys
that still frame
the future
 I dreamed

The Autobiography of Poverty

In places
where the poor
dared to romp
I journeyed there
to deposit
my hope
where I find it
even today
where poverty
can't touch
nor confiscate

The Banquet of the Dispossessed

House of the Mortally Poor

The Pied Piper played
And we danced to solemn rites
That had no melody
For ours was a life
Punctuated by ambiguities
Last hired
First fired
Felony convictions
For misdemeanor crimes
Education deferred to illiteracy
Truancy
Low-test scores
Future left behind
Minimum wage
Maximum fines
Low income
No income
Unemployment lines
High risk factors
Excuses never defined
Violence at the front door
Swindlers at the back

The Autobiography of Poverty

Bullies
Dope heads
Brain dead on crack

Ghetto cartels
Meth deals gone bad
Drug busts
Drive-by pushers
Turning tricks for fast cash
Turf wars
Bullets flying
Pimps and prostitutes
Addiction
Affliction
Underage recruits
Police brutality
Cover-ups
Slaying of the innocent
Cops on the take
Jails in walking distance

Hung over
Hanging out
Hung out to dry
Nicknames reinforce bondage
No tears to cry
Thug
Ice man
Mad Dog
Bad Willie

The Autobiography of Poverty

Hoochie
Baby Mama
Raging
Restless River

Anger played out in crimes of futility
Armed robbery
Theft by taking
Breaking and entering
Petty theft
Petty larceny
Auto vandalism

Theft of service
Substance abuse
Selling of children
Pan-handling
Parole violations
Pawning stolen jewelry

The Pied Piper played its requiem of regret
And we danced
To the ongoing fate of neglect
Nohyphennocommanocolonorperiod
Wejustdancedanddancedanddancedtodelirium

Shawty
Sleepy
Peeping but not seeing

The Autobiography of Poverty

Half Pint
Little Joe
Need-Mo stability

Life scattered from jail to jail
Shelter to shelter eviction
Living out of bags
Carts
And soup kitchens

Future marked and marred
By too much
Or too little
Too many bills
Too many children
Too much time lost
Too much trial and error
Too far from tomorrow
Too close to the past
Too many worries
Too much of no class

So we danced
To the power of the unrelenting
No admittance
No vacancies
No trespassing
No children

No experience
No resume
No truth in the media
No brother
Or sister
No parent or guardian

Just havens of insufficiencies
Consumers
And borrowers
Brown paper bags
To drown our sorrows

Insufficient this
insufficient that
insufficient funds
Insufficient credit
Insufficient references
Insufficient education
Insufficiently competent
insufficient dedication

Unqualified
Undignified
Unwanted baggage
Uneducated
Unemployed
Unrepresented Americans

The Autobiography of Poverty

Scorned for the audacity
To breathe the air
Of the living
Dreams sabotaged
By gross inabilities

Can't read
Can't write
Can't afford it
Can't fix it
Disregarded and subjected
To discriminating existence

Disqualified
Disdained
Disabled
Disrespected
Distrusted
Disenfranchised
Sold to in "as is" condition
Then barred from fair trading
Except consumerism

Cyclical abuse
No truth in lending
No exchange
No refund
Warranty limited
Penalties for being late
And over the limit
High interest for low living

The Autobiography of Poverty

So the pied piper played his requiem of regret
And we danced to the ongoing fate of neglect

Nohyphennocommanocolonorperiod
Wejustdancedanddancedanddancedtodelerium

We danced to defective and dysfunctional contentment
Lives clogged like toilets exposed to sewage injection
Iron broke
Doors off the hinges
Rats
Roaches
No gas or electricity

Day after day
Freewheeling to disaster
Free lunch
Free housing
Free legal counsel

Case lost by default
And lack of interest
Future shipwrecked
By never ending conditions

No bond
No driver's license
No tags or registration

The Autobiography of Poverty

No bus fare
No fuel
No phone
Or nearest relative

No social security card
No green card
No English
No savings
No trust funds
No sponsor
No voter's registration

No show moms
No good dads
No bonds for education
No G.E.D
No S.A.T
No college applications
No benefits
No child support
No alimony
No custody
No babysitter
No parental interference

No concerned neighbor
No continuance
No exceptions

No re-entrance
No outlet
No outright contesting

Dead-end boredom
Stifling and unchecked
Rendering unfruitful
Nowhere to vent

No regrets
No hunger
No thirst for tomorrow
Never the lender
Always the borrower

Genius aborted
Languishing on the vine
Potential substituted
For the sport of the maligned
Shooting craps
Pipe dreaming
Left to fantasize
Hope in a bottle
Never realized

Lotteries
Casinos
Chancing and hoping
Odds overwhelming
Depression
No coping

The Autobiography of Poverty

Rappers on the corner
J-Z hopefuls
Pimping and pushing
Over doping
Wasting time
For a toss and a chance
No specific dream
No alternate plan

Barriers imposed
Three Strikes You're Out
Life without Parole
No second chance
No Pardon
No credit for trying
No will
No insurance
No preparation for dying

No access
No exit
Imposed death convictions
Penalized for passing
Through the land of the living

Living the lie
On the stallion of delusion
The American dream
Filled with hope and confusion
Designed only for those
So inclined
Who live above the poverty line

The rest is a dare
An arduous journey
Casting off the stigma
Of the impecunious

Still they dance
Wrapped in frolic and frivolity
Climbing stairs in the dark
Crossing waters without paddles

Taxation without representation
In the system that fails
Fighting against the odds
Pulling their dreams uphill

Satan in the foreground
Pharaoh at the back
No power to continue
Or the will to counteract

Fasting and prayer
But no true repentance
Living in hell
Calling on Jesus
Using religion as a crutch
Rather than a ladder
Losing the war
Trying to win the battle

The Autobiography of Poverty

Straddling the fence
Rather than to climb it
Resolute in the moment
Damned for trying

Consulting with the dead
To guide their living
Gambling away good money
On bad investments
Throwing paycheck
After paycheck
Up a wild hog's behind
With no way to trace
Where the hog lies down

Ill-gotten schemes
Scattered by the wind
Drug money
Fencing
For a future
That doesn't exist

The pied piper played its requiem of regret
And we danced to the ongoing fate of neglect

Nohyphennocommanocolonorperiod
Wejustdancedanddancedanddancedtodelirium

Solution unavailable
Except we die trying

The Eugenics Conspiracy

The day they marched
For voting rights
Mudd sat across
From a social worker
Seeking assistance
For ten children
The plump black woman
Had no sympathy
Shuffling the papers
To coerce Mudd's signature

Trying to convince her
That another child
Was one too many
But Uncle Sam
Had the answer
If she cooperated

The poor
Illiterate
The mentally ill
Shouldn't be permitted
To reproduce
Inferior offspring

The Autobiography of Poverty

The plan in place
She qualified
Charge it to
Bureaucratic
Genocide

While Annie Cooper
Was being beat
And scarred
Mudd flung that binder
Across the room
And told that "hussy"
In no uncertain terms
To shove those papers
Where the sun never shines

Until I know for certain
For certain that I am not
I have one husband
I have one God
No one will control
The fruit of my loins

Besides
I'm having these children
For God
And no one but God
Can decide their future

Then she marched
Six-month pregnant
Anger flaring
Like a Civil Rights Activist
Marched
Through neighborhoods
Of giggling children
Home alone
While parents earned a living
And soldiers marched
For their freedom

The first to die

Cotton

The Coronation of the American Dream

Snoring yields to snoozing
The cacophonies of the night are stilled
There are no sounds astir the shotgun house
Except the arousing pleas
And the apologetic sighs
Of the keeper of the children
Breathing morning mist
Silhouetted against the slumber
Of mill town malaise
Preempting our rest
At 4am Christmas Eve

We pray that these are just
The fading images of dawn
Suspended between
Whistling snores and the cricket's
Song

But our hopes are dashed
Humbling to the dismal white
Of December frost
Settling beneath our bones

Chilling
Unsympathetically cold

As mom calls us name by name

Tom
Louise
Dorse Jean
Frances
Walter
Chester Ray
Nancy!

It's not a dream
It's the reality of shame
Dignity lost
In the celebration of poverty
Performed from town to town
Bowing to the King Pin of the South

Adorned by indignities
Heaped upon slaves
"Pickaninnies"
and Coloreds
Iniquity crowned
By the sweat of the brow

We shuffle our regrets from foot to foot
Scoot over the paint peeled tailgate
Of Mr. William's disgraceful pickup

Yesterday's hunger still denied
Until 10AM Eastern Standard Time

Toboggan heads
Nylon socks for mittens
Flesh
Flushed against flesh to keep warm

Feet
Mummified in burlap sacks
Tailored to feet
Compliments of daddy's hawk blade knife

Designed to war against thirty miles
Of treacherous winter
On the way to Bailey
Bethel
Wilson or
Eureka

Wind chill stabbing in the nose
Like a blunt icicle
Delaying circulation
Leaving the body a lethargic heap
Of numb chattel property

All for cotton

Soft
Gentle
Seductive white
Virgin meringue fantasies
Trapped between
Hulls
And briars

Alluring to the eye
Deceiving to the touch

Pricking

Entangling lies

Like the American dream

Hope ensnared by thistles
Progress
Sabotaged by delusions
Now left behind

Fingers
Exposed to the elements
Frostbitten
Sacrificed to cotton
Evoking expository murmuring
The dream turn nightmare
Right before our eyes

Children
Pleading to be exempt
Spared the indignity of snot
Nasal mucus
Frozen across the lip
Like a Revlon mask unpeeled

The Autobiography of Poverty

Grown folk
Breathing out expletives
Swearing
Cussing
Threatening to quit by nine

Bump this s_ _t
I'm out of here

Working up sweat translates to warmth
Until options narrow to capitulation
Yield to reticence
Then
Silence
Epiphanies of the by and by
Bursts of inspiration

Hope compromised for consolation
Pie in the sky

Then Mudd breaks out into a work song

There's a bright side somewhere
There's a bright side somewhere
Don't you rest until you find it
There's a bright side somewhere

Unisom
Harmony
A cappella

Cotton
Lulling into complacency
To accept that which for now
Must be

Then one day
Soon and very soon
We're going where Jesus is
In a moment
In the blink of an eye
We shall be changed

And ain't no cotton
Gonna hold
My body down

Honey child
Hush your mouth!
Ain't no cotton
Gonna hold
My body down

Laughter
Hard
Harder

Cathartic
Free
If but for a moment

The Autobiography of Poverty

But Lawdy today

We need Ms. Cotton

The bale of the ball
So we can buy shoes
School books
Three months overdue

And if God's watching
A pot of beef stew
With carrots this time

God's too good to let me down

Cotton
A winter trick
Played on the poor

Or a blessing
Wrapped in swaddling

So we can get Christmas
Out of layaway
Mudd's ring out of hock

At four cents a pound
That's four dollars a hundred
It comes right down
To what's more important

The Autobiography of Poverty

Rent
Kerosene
Vittles on the table
Light to live by

Maybe

Unless it rains
And cotton swells

Then we'll have Christmas
Thick
Like syrup from cane
Heavy
Like dancing rain

Weightier
Than the cold of poor folks
Pain

Like presoaked washing in a sable pot
Proud
Like Southern bales
Flaunted by the masters
At the county fair

Peaking at twenty-nine
To tip the scales of the planters
Until old boll weevil
Smeared her crown

The Autobiography of Poverty

And we worked harder

Just to have supper
Or a crimson red bike
Between ten children

Pick up sticks
Jump ropes too short
And bobby socks
One size fits all

Cheap Lincoln logs
And stringy haired white dolls
With pop out limbs
Threatening to disintegrate
By Three O'clock

Unless it rains

Then we'll have Christmas
White folk Christmas
Fit for kings

A chicken roast
A three-dollar tree
Real banana pudding
Maybe ice cream
Or egg nod

The Autobiography of Poverty

A five-hundred-piece jigsaw puzzle
Depicting landscapes
Unattainable
Fading into the sunset
Of the American dream

While we sing praises to the lord
For the blessing we receive
Rejection
Scraps of tangled tinsel
A languid tree
Tossed to and fro
Like we
Shielding ten brown paper bags
From A&P

Names scribbled across the fold
In crayon

Bearing our hopes
From White Santa

The Autobiography of Poverty

Apples
Oranges
Peanut Brittle
Walnuts
Pecans
And the promise of cotton

Joy to the world
The lord has come
Let earth receive her king

Let all of its pomp and glory shine
But thank God for the rain

The Food that Angels Bring

Thank you Lord
For a meal
I am not choosey
Just grateful
That the place once empty
Is now filled
And I can sleep
Without the rumbling
That keeps me awake
Wondering
If tomorrow
Will be any different
Than today

Sell or Discard by Friday

Piles
Bunches
Ceiling high
Icings overrun
Chocolate cupcakes
Vanilla sandwiches
Strawberry zingers
Days old
Stale bread
Buns
Rolls
Waiting to be devoured
By
Indiscriminate
Mouths
Breakfast
Lunch
Whenever

Butterflies and Bean Cans

I cross my fingers
when there is a reason
to hope
that tonight we might not have
pork and beans
and wieners

I cross my fingers
and wait...
until time runs out
and there is nothing left
but a prayer
that Mudd will make it
before O'Neal's Market
closes

I wait
only to hear
the rusty knife
stumbling
around the top
of cans
without labels

The Autobiography of Poverty

And the sound of pig
being abducted
from jagged edge foil

Without protest
again
and I am so grateful
my stomach
dances a jig

Library Rules

The Dewey Decimal System
Didn't work for us that day
We were misfiled misfits
According to race
Or not filed at all
Just because
We were black
But if we hurry
We can gather pecans
To sell at market
There are four of us
And just one lot

Like Leprechauns
We scramble
Across the lawn
Of manicured trees
Back and forth
To a bag
Sitting in a strategic place

The Autobiography of Poverty

Stuffing our pockets
Between trips
To make the most of time
But the librarian's warning
Reverberates between the trees
"Get out!"
Or I will call the police
And just as quickly as we had hoped
We bolt across the parking lot
And abandoned our dream
In the middle of the yard
For fear
The spooky spinster
 Would make good her threat

That four black children
Were stealing pecans
From the public ground
Where they pay taxes

We kick our disgust
Beneath our feet of dead leaves
Along the homeward path

Gnawing on defeat
Refusing to swallow
Keeping steady pace
With the growling soundtrack
Of hunger songs
Trapped in the belly

We Stumble over uneven pavement
Which beckons our glance downward
All around the parking lot
A block away from denied
Pecans covered the ground

And in quick haste delight
God redeemed our shame
In bulging pockets
Of skirts
And pants
Pressed down
Shaken together
In victory

Just before
The market closed
We met Mr. O'Neal at the door
He bought pecans
We bought flour
And redeemed our dignity
With food songs

Shadows on the Ceiling

Excerpts: The Poverty Manifesto, 2005

We were not as poor as some
still poorer than others
but you can't imagine the extremes
unless you've lived it
breathed it
absorbed its existence

Cold in winter
no wood burning stove
not enough kindling
no ceiling or floor fan
or air conditioner
no breeze summers

You have to eat it
or not eat at all
bland blackeye peas
the guts of hogs
unsalted rice
government cheese
shared with house mice

Saltine crackers
barely enough peanut butter
to quench tasteless hunger
appetite curbed
by scarcity and crumbs
stomachs growling
invoking the help of the merciful
whoever
whatever
borrowing
begging
stealing
doing anything
to avoid another day of empty

Returning bottles for deposits
or pecans in exchange for beans
picking up scraps from the ground
from trash receptacles
or dumping fields
to hold together the pretense
or
delusion of being filled
encrusted ice
bits and pieces
of this and that
found here and there

The Autobiography of Poverty

Clay dirt
or discarded candy
violated
beneath the feet
an occasional surprise
happens upon those
who yearn

Stale buns and rolls
charity
for houses without means
jobs that don't pay
eyes that look
and glare into the face
but cannot see
the vastness of despair
simply because
they don't live there

You cannot imagine
what it is like
to be nameless
you must dwell there
among roaches
concealed
behind cheap frames
and furniture
or in plain view

The Autobiography of Poverty

Reclining on sofas
or crawling across the wall
in no hurry to leave
their abode
racing for your supper
or whatever left to disease
competing for life
courting
necking
frolicking in squalor
brazenly cohabitating
mating
hatching their young
to reign in the filth they breed
knowing as much about you
as you know about yourself

Stowaways in the pockets
and the legs of trousers
making their lifeless debut
unexpectedly
squished between the pages of history
that showcase dynasties
or still alive

Crawling inconspicuously
unabashedly
seeking familiarity
which they find
under the sole of the shoe

The Autobiography of Poverty

Rites of disgust
where they die
for abuse of hospitality
their testimony silenced
Inadmissible shame
before they expose
our indignities
in the company
of strangers

Have you lived behind
the panes of poverty
where
cardboard dreams
suffice for broken windows
never replaced
and pots and pans without lids
substitute for China
utensils

and labels
property
of the US Department
of Agricultural
"Not for resale"
punishable by law
because by birth of being
you violated
the basic fundamental
code of human decency

Thereby
you're sentenced to a life of
canned pork and gravy
powder eggs
dry milk
blocks of cheese
peanut Butter
and split peas

Have you ever lived
where poverty inhabits
no frills
just make-believe
fantasies
no curb appeal
hope only to those
who dare believe
who do not digest
quit
or
die
prematurely

The Autobiography of Poverty

Have you ever slept
where poverty sleeps
two beds
between ten children
legs dangling over jagged
box springs
where second-hand mattresses
form shapes that we read
in urine patterns
we can breathe in
exhale
or imagine
they are the fantasies
of places
we have no right
to dream

Or will ever belong
because poverty
has no teacher
who mentors the dreamer
except
we pray
that the shadows
on the ceilings
will reach down
and pull us upward

Or call us forth
from an environment
that takes hostages
unapologetically
where hope dies in the womb
like the embryos
of unwanted pregnancies
ripped from the body
by homemade devices
void of caring
where one mouth to feed
is too many
and one more
is the abuse of humanity

Where babies are born
deprived of fight
because of apathy
ignorance
or deficit living
chances for survival
sabotaged by numbers
SIDS
malnutrition
sexually transmitted diseases
(Gonorrhea, Syphilis, Herpes, Crabs, AIDS)
or miscarried
intentionally
or by mistake

The Autobiography of Poverty

Abusing alcohol
and drug addiction
smoke inhalation
in the placenta

Have you ever lived
behind walls and fences
of squalor slums
paint peeled ceilings
boarded and vacant buildings
bathroom next to kitchens
unsanitary without permission
trash cans
and uncovered garbage
kicked
or flung against the curbs
like the rejected lives of their breeders
putrefying………….
repulsive
doors ripped from the hinges
inviting vandals
accommodating useless relatives
and nosey neighbors at will

Do you know the grief
of sitting on
damp hardwood floors
with holes opened to mice
water bugs and
land contaminates

~~Or windows shattered~~
like hope
covered with plastic
leaky roofs
clogged drains
toilets that ~~won't flush~~
utilities ~~dis~~connected
for days and weeks
while slum landlords
close their eyes
destitute of sympathy

Aiding and abetting
in the breeding of poverty
and affective disorders
pathogenic matter
invading
biting
gnawing through the skin
infecting to diseased pores
dying for lack of attention

Or not…
depending on
the mind of the keeper
who stands watch
with determination
to disarm our complicity
to shame
and premature dying

The Autobiography of Poverty

Put your hand on your heart
She commands
I shall live and not die
He that walks with the wise
shall be wise
but a companion of fools
shall be destroyed...
The Lord is my shepherd
I shall not want
Our Father
Give us this day
Our daily bread
Amen
Good night
Thank the Lord

If God is for us
who can stand against us
we might live in poverty
but
poverty doesn't live in us
on and on
drilling beneath the conscious
of reality
building a wall of resistance
to fear
and resilience
to scale barriers
designed to imprison

The Autobiography of Poverty

You can't imagine poverty
that doesn't cover indignities
you would have to live its ragged
naked narrative
clothes tattered
from constant wearing
homemade
hand-me-downs
rummage sales
existence

Thrift shop soiled
dingy
grimy
wearing other folk lives
year to year
ring around the collar
offensive
repelling potential friends
baggy and beltless
tight-fitting
belonging to a younger sibling
oversized
or worn backwards
to deceive yesterday's scrutiny
a feast spread
for bullies

The Autobiography of Poverty

You can't even see it
unless you've worn poverty
upon your feet
or walked miles in shoes
without soles
too cramped
or toes
exposed
to freezing
because your feet outgrew them
last winter
or they were passed down
or picked up
from heaps of trash
or some swap meet madness

shoes cut out at the toe
to relieve corns
calluses
bunions
and in-grown toenails
toes exposed to the elements
(rocks with jagged edges, stumps, mud, water puddles, inclement
weather, winter cold, insects, and critters)
frost bitten or numb
feet swelling
protesting to deafness
soles detached from body
limp and lifeless
DOA

Flapping haphazardly
serving no purpose
except to disgrace
throwing off the rhythm of life
slowing progress
revealing cardboard stuffed
humiliation
barefoot
the ultimate protest of living in crisis

Have you ever walked
lived
bathed
or existed
with morbid looming shadows
where squished candles
serve to illuminate
a darkness filled with pretenses
and salt
is the multipurpose substitute
for everything hygienic
toothpaste
deodorant
soap for stench
or medicinal
intervention
to prevent
infection
from the malady
of less fortunate

The Autobiography of Poverty

Separated
dispossessed
from all that's basic
to human survival
plunging into distress
moving from hunger to starvation
enduring heat to sweltering
piercing the flesh to mold
coldness that refrigerates the pores
to deadness

Where cheap space heaters and candles
babysit the night
until inadvertently kicked over
and engulf hope
devouring the future
in flames
leaving homeless
with no redress

Possessions flung to the curb
confiscated
privacy sprawled
across frigid pavements
humanity demeaned
forced into nomadic pilgrimage
life suspended
temporarily
or permanently

In alleys
under viaducts and bridges
shelters and soup kitchens
street corners
squatting
in condemned property
and homes of relatives
or strangers
void of warmth and caring

Dejected and displaced
stowaways
runaways
hitching rides to their destines
DFACS
prostitution
and pornographic living
foster homes
gangs
jails
and park benches

Juvenile detention
bus stations
storefront churches
travelling circuses
cults
shelters
mental hospitals

Crack houses
safe houses
pimps and pushers
ditches
junkyards
abandoned vehicles

Until finally
morgues
caretakers of the departed
whether suicide
homicide
or accidental

Hunger
abuse
parental neglect
careless
overdoses
government tampering
domestic feuding
crimes of passion
restless violence
incestuous cover-ups
lack of insurance
or temporary madness
under the strain of living

The Autobiography of Poverty

Mind ravished
by defective decisions
predisposed
to an undiagnosed condition
there is no lithium
for those
who do not know
that poverty
is their affliction

Hopelessness
defeatism
and causes unknown
except
Hattie Mae
is your mother
then death
by giving up
is not an option

Places Called Home

The tapestry chairs must go
they have found a new home
back in the showroom
or on the sidewalk
among strangers
rummaging
through other folk privacies

The Formica top dining table
that comfortably sat six
energetic conversationalists
will hold its memorial
along the side of the road
to be gawked at by neighbors
waiting for nightfall
to plunder the remains
of what once was home

Scavengers
who lack sensitivity
for other folk misfortunes
will hold their vigils
under the cover of dark
until they've fed
their famished curiosity full
with inanimate narratives

This is no longer our gathering place
for laughter
and dance
celebratory of family
it holds no intimate value
we are estranged
we must not cling
to sentimentalities

Ritual of Humiliation

I do not want to go to school today
the crackers won't stick
not enough peanut butter
between four children
and I do not have
three cents for milk
or a note from Mudd
to pay next week

By lunch
the crackers will be separated
in a soiled brown
paper bag
for lack of cohesion
like what I feel inside

Dry

Empty

And Lula Moore
in a jealous rage
just might attack
my lunch again

And I will not have
the strength I need
to return
her anger

Because the crackers
wouldn't stick
and I don't have
three cents for milk

Blackberry Dreams

The beauty around me speaks
It's not poverty that confounds me
It's the serenade of morning
"Come, the day rises to meet you"
I am greeted with the wonder of sounds
And sights to my delight

A red belly blue bird
Chirps along a trail
and the squish sound
Of pure blackberries
Being crushed
Beneath my feet

I pick them from the vine
The black-purple juices
Flow to the tips of my finger
I gently press them to my lips
Savoring the joy of nature
To be baked in a Sunday pie
And gulped down after church

That is
If we can make it
Before the thunderstorms
And pouring rains
Overtake us

Oops
There tucked in the green
Is sweet grass
Tender and eatable
I pull it up
Into my mouth

"Dorse Jean!
Get up
Or, we'll be late for Sunday School"
I stretch and yawn
Yawn and stretch
The jagged-edge box springs
Scratch my scrawny legs
I know we will have oatmeal
Again today

But
I am glad to smell
The creamy curl
Of oats bathing
In yellow butter
Sprinkled with sugar
And blackberry syrup

That will roll over my tongue
Like a silky long trail
That I will walk and relive
And relish
Time
And time again

The Parable of One

Dorse Jean

How many houses can the rich own

As many as their money is long, ma'am

And how many houses can the rich occupy

One, ma'am

Dorse Jean

How many cars can the rich procure

As many as they can afford, I guess, ma'am

And how many cars can the rich drive

Just one at a time, ma'am

Just one at a time

The Autobiography of Poverty

Dorse Jean

How many pairs of shoes can the rich hoard

Hundreds or even thousands, I suppose, ma'am

And how many pairs can the rich wear

One pair at a time, ma'am

Dorse Jean

How many countries can the r ich enjoy

As many as they have the time and money for

And in how many can he live his earth life

Just one house at a time, ma'am

Dorse Jean

How many lifetimes cant the rich live

One life one day at a time

I'm certain, ma'am

The Autobiography of Poverty

Dorse Jean

How many lives can the rich buy

None, ma'am

Because they don't own the breath

Dorse Jean

How many deaths will the rich die

One death, ma'am

Someday, somehow

When their days are numbered

They too will die

Afterword

Everybody's Talking about Hattie Mae's Children Again

Do y'all remember
Hattie Mae's Children
The ones we thought
Wouldn't amount to nothing

Well…
I heard
And this ain't gossip
I saw it on television
And it's the gospel

Hattie Mae's children
Branded themselves
"House of Wellington"
Imagine that

Lawyers
PhDs
Masters in Psychology
and Philosophy

A record breaking
R&B singer
TV stars
And a top brass banker
A major in the Air Force
A jewelry maker
Published authors
A museum curator

Gospel globe trotters
Tech geniuses
Couture designers
Motivational speakers

Thespians
Movie Stars
Movers and shakers
Mentors
Educators
History makers

Apostles
Prophets
Diviners of Dreams
Preachers
Teachers

Can you believe it?

They spun their narratives
Against the odds
Hattie Mae's children
Have evolved
From cotton fields
And tobacco shacks
Cucumber mills
And burlap sacks

To places thought
Too high to reach
Except they refused
To concede defeat

Hattie Mae
Was no joke herself
"I'm having these children
for God"
She declared

She gave them a dream
In the midst of poverty
And wings of faith
To soar above it
"Poverty" she declared
"Is a state of mind;
It's only your destiny
If YOU give it power"
(Period)

So she led the way
Became the drum major
That led the band
And inspired them higher

You have a peculiar way with words
You could be a writer
Use your next quarter
To buy more pencils
I think
As I compose
This next verse
Aspiring to win
The Pulitzer Prize

That's good drawing
So she entered Nancy's name
Into a summer art course
And here she is
AA, BA, MFA, a PhD later
in her chosen profession

You have the hands of a beautician
I can't even feel them
As you massage my scalp
So she became
A state certified instructor
In the art of cosmetology

Fueling our dreams
until every goal
Capitulated
At our feet

And so we won
State forensics
In spoken word
A full scholarship
To VA Polytechnical

Then at forty-eight
Modeling the resilience
She instilled
She studied and received
Her GED

At seventy-one
Still not finished
She achieved her goal
And enrolled in Spelman

There was never a challenge
She couldn't overcome
By precept
And example
She came
She lived
She conquered

Doris Wellington

Former American University student, and independent scholar, Doris Wellington, is an ordained minister, community organizer, social activist, visionary poet, playwright, author, publisher, dream analyst, and inspirational speaker. Born in Bull Head Township, North Carolina, she is the third of eleven children gifted to poor migrant sharecroppers, Luther and Hattie Vance-Wellington. Her great grandfather, Frank Worthington, escaped from a Pitt County, NC plantation and joined the United States Colored Troops of the Union Army, December 12, 1864. To honor his epic achievement, she wrote the epic poetry tribute, Soldier X: From Escaped Slave to the Civil War.

She received the American University Scholarship in Community Studies and studied from 1981-1984 before accepting an invitation to travel abroad for Missions work, which turned into a fulltime profession crisscrossing the nation and abroad with the message of the Gospel. She has conducted ten ministry tours abroad as well as ministry in thirty states in the United States. She founded House of Wellington, Inc. to inspire and launch four generations of family music, art, and entrainment, which produced the first nationally toured hip-hop stage play.

Her creative inspiration is the marriage of eight interwoven life portals—a religious upbringing, the supernatural world of dreams and visions, childhood poverty, the faith of a resilient warrior mother, a sensitivity to mental illness, love and its intrinsic nature to both pain and pleasure, the African American illusion of freedom, and the ongoing enlightenment of the perilous experiences as a woman, specifically a black woman challenged in the socio-political framework as the other in the United States of America.

Her literary focus is issue-specific epic poems, stage productions, films, and books of various genres. She founded Dwelling Places Publisher to independently platform her body of work.

She has authored, twenty epic stage plays, including the celebrated allegorical production, *I Waltzed with God the Morning of Genesis: A Mosaic for Peace, Dead Woman Dancing on Her Grave*, and *God, I'm Here and I'm Colored: the National Debate on Race and Equality*. She is the author of the thirteen-book poetic epistolary, *Romancing God: The Divine Love Affair*; as well as *The Divine Notebook: Letters*, and *The Poverty Manifesto*.

Additionally, she has authored four novels, and one memoir, *The River God Runs through Her*. She coauthored *Stokestown: Dreaming behind Closed Doors.*, 2015. She has recorded and studied more than 20,000 prophetic dreams, visions and supernatural visitations. She founded and wrote the curriculum for **The Prophetic Path Dream Summit**, which teaches the prophetically inclined how to tap into the hidden power of dreams.

She is the Founding Director of The Great Commission Humanitarian Project, which focuses on mental health wellness, social justice, humanitarianism, poverty and homelessness, and issues involving disenfranchised women and girls, including but not limited to: sex trafficking, domestic abuse, rape, bullying via social media, racism, sexual harassment, and other socially exclusive and socially damaging issues.

Doris Wellington travels internationally as a minister and motivational speaker.

Dwelling Places Worldwide
Home of Books and Letters
By Doris Wellington

Amazon.com, Createspace.com, BarnesandNoble.com
and other online and retail booksellers

The River God Runs through Her: Praise for an unlikely Champion
Stokestown: Dreaming behind Closed Doors
Romancing God: the Divine Love Affair Volumes Series
The Poverty Manifesto: Satire, Soliloquy, Sentiments
I Waltzed with God the Morning of Genesis: Peace and the Humanity of Gods
Songs and Sermons of the Pentecostal Sabbath
Rhapsody for September: Love Letters
Winter's Dark, A Love Story
The Divine Notebook
The Dear John Reader: Rituals of Self Disclosure in Love
and Emotional Emancipation
Dead Woman Dancing on Her Grave: Unstoppable
Woman in a Jar: Narratives of a Perfect Insanity
God, I'm Here and I'm Colored: the National Debate on Race & Equality
The Hurt Café: How to Have a Breakdown without Going Crazy
The Sharecropper's Muse
Narratives of Abuse and the Abdication of Shame

*Until we tell our own truth in our own voices; we will remain victims—
faceless and silent on the pages of a history never written.
Thus, there are stories that must be told; codes of silence that must be broken.*
Doris Wellington

www.ingramcontent.com/pod-product-compliance
Lightning Source LLC
Chambersburg PA
CBHW050113170426
43198CB00014B/2564